THE
MIGHTY WARRIORS

SAM HOUSTON
Champion
of
AMERICA

by
ALLAN CARPENTER

Rourke Publications Inc.
Vero Beach, Florida 32964

EDITORIAL ACKNOWLEDGMENTS
Illustrations
WESLEY KLUG
Assistant to the Author
and Indexer
CARL PROVORSE
Typography by
LAW BULLETIN PUBLISHING COMPANY

Published by Rourke Publications, Inc.
Vero Beach, FL 32964

Library of Congress Cataloging-in-Publication Data
Carpenter, Allan, 1917-
    Sam Houston, Champion of America.
    (The Mighty Warriors)
    Bibliography: P. 98
    Includes index.
    Summary: A biography of the colorful Sam Houston
who served America in many ways, but whose name is
now inextricably linked with Texas.
    1. Houston, Sam, 1793-1863—Juvenile literature.
2. Texas—Governors—Biography—Juvenile literature. 3. Legislators—United States—Biography—Juvenile literature. 4. United States. Congress. Senate—Biography—Juvenile literature. [1. Houston,
Sam, 1793-1863. 2. Governors] I. Title. II. Series:
Carpenter, Allan, 1917- . Mighty Warriors.
F390.H84C37 1987 976.4'04'0924 [B] [92] 87-9688
ISBN O-86625-327-0

Preceding pages, the Battle of San Jacinto was one of the most
important in world history, famed painting by H. A. Mc Cardle.

CONTENTS

The lieutenant pulled the arrow out, along with a great chunk of flesh, and Sam Houston went back into the battle, painting by Wesley Klug.

Chapter One

BARBED ARROWS AND BULLETS

He felt the sharp pain as the arrow plunged into his thigh. He tried to pull it out, but it was lined with barbs that tore against his flesh. On March 27, 1814, as the battle with the Indians raged, he asked a lieutenant to pull the arrow out. When the lieutenant suggested that he go to the field doctor, the wounded man drew his sword and commanded the lieutenant to pull out the terrible projectile.

Tugging with all his might, the lieutenant ripped out the arrow along with great chunks of flesh. Just then the commander himself, General Andrew Jackson, came up and ordered the wounded man to leave the battle. However, he disregarded this command. As soon as a doctor had stopped the bleeding, he jumped up and led his platoon against the last stronghold of the Indians in the Battle of Horseshoe Bend.

Just as he reached the top of the Indians' fortification, two bullets struck him, and for Sam Houston the War of 1812 was over.

Army doctors cared for Houston's arrow wound. They managed to dig out one of the bullets in his shoulder. Because he seemed so near death the doctors did not even try to pull out the other bullet; they left Sam Houston on the battlefield with the bodies of the dead and those who were dying.

The next day Sam was still alive, so the medics strapped him to a carrying litter made of tree branches, and they dragged him to an army fort sixty miles away. There he seemed so near death that, again, little was done to help him. But Sam was determined to cling to life. Sam suffered for two years before doctors in New Orleans were finally able to remove the other bullet. His shoulder remained sore and painful all the rest of his life.

This incident was just one of the many in Sam Houston's life that demonstrate his courage, pride, determination and patriotism. These qualities served him well. They also played an important part in the story of his country.

Sam Houston was a great patriot who always put the good of the United States ahead of his own interests. This staunch loyalty may have kept him from realizing his greatest ambition: to become President of the United States.

Although he never became a U.S. president, Sam Houston served in more high positions than any other person in American history. He was twice elected president of an independent nation. He served as governor of two different states. He was the commanding general of an army. He became an ambassador to Washington. He served as a United States Senator and also in the U.S. House of Representatives. He held many other important posts as well.

They carried him on a litter.

Chapter Two

BEGINNINGS

This unique life began in a small, rustic log cabin near Lexington, Virginia. There Samuel Houston was born on March 2, 1793, the fifth of a family of nine children.

Sam believed that his "indomitable courage" came from his father, Major Sam Houston, an inspector of militia. The senior Sam traveled around Virginia on his military duties. Then he sold his Virginia farm, bought 419 acres of Tennessee land and decided to move to his new purchase. But Major Houston died before the move could be made. Sam, junior, was thirteen at the time.

With her Virginia home sold, Elizabeth Paxton Houston carried out her husband's plans. She packed up her brood and moved by wagon to a new home in Blount County, Tennessee, near Maryville.

Sam loved his mother and admired her "...intellectual and moral qualities...and stern fortitude." However, he hated life on their farm. He was bossed by his four older brothers. He had little time to read the books about early Greek heroes and other great books the family had brought with them from Virginia. He thought those heroes and others like them were wonderful. He wanted to be like them some day.

Sam always seemed to like the underdog, the person or group that made enemies at home or heroes who faced great odds. One of his favorite heroes of ancient times was Caius Marius. Marius had been born in a humble Roman family. He rose to high rank in Rome. Then he was forced into exile during one of Rome's many civil wars. Sam admired the way he fought back. He particularly liked the bold way Marius defeated the Numidians and Teutons.

Sam, too, had begun with a humble position in life. But the lives of his heroes gave him many examples of how humble people could rise to great places, serving their country.

When Sam proved to be of little help on the family farm, his brothers insisted that he get a job. So Sam went to work in the town store, but he hated that life even more. When he was fifteen Sam ran away from home.

He did what many boys have often thought of doing. He went to stay with the Cherokee Indians who lived on an island in the Tennessee River. The Indians called him Co-lo-neh, meaning raven, and the raven became his symbol. He learned the Cherokee language and customs, including their hunting methods. During his three year stay, Sam was adopted by Chief Oo-loo-te-ka as his own son. Today the chief is perhaps better known as John Jolly, the name he used among white people.

Sam's brothers often tried to get him to come back home. Although Sam returned home several times, he always went back to his Indian friends—after borrowing money to buy gifts to take back to them!

Sam allowed these gift debts to reach the sum of $100. In those days this was a large amount of money. So Sam went back to "civilization" to earn money to pay back his debts. He had no real formal education. Nevertheless, he opened a school, charging eight dollars per term. He taught until he had paid his debts.

On March 24, 1813, army recruiters marched into Maryville with drums rumbling and banners streaming. The recruiters threw a handful of silver dollars on one of the drums. Those who wanted to

Opposite, Sam ran away to live with the Indians, took an Indian name and learned Indian ways and customs, painting by Wesley Klug.

join the army were told to pick up one of the dollars. Sam picked up a dollar and joined the army, hoping to become a hero.

When he left home, Sam's mother gave him a ring with the word *honor* engraved on the inside. For the rest of his life, Sam Houston wore the ring and tried to live up to the motto.

Chapter Three

SOLDIER AND POLITICIAN

Samuel Houston's participation in the War of 1812 began and ended with the Battle of Horseshoe Bend. It was in this conflict with the Red Sticks Indians that he was heroically wounded and left for dead.

The War of 1812 had been going on for more than two years when this battle started. By this time Sam had become an ensign in charge of a platoon. On March 27, 1814, the great general Andrew Jackson had lined up his forces behind a mound of earth that served as a rampart. The group of Creek Indians known as Red Sticks had supported the British, and Jackson was determined to conquer them. Sam's platoon was lined up with the others, waiting to attack the Indians.

The Red Sticks were fairly well armed with

rifles as well as bows and arrows. They had made a rough fort out of logs. Others were hiding behind the trees. When the Americans attacked the fortress, Major Lemuel P. Montgomery was killed at once. Right behind him was Ensign Sam Houston, leading his platoon. The army managed to storm the stronghold, and the battle became a series of smaller clashes.

It was then that Sam Houston received the wounds which troubled him all the rest of his life.

Strangely, this was the only battle in which Houston took part until he led another army group into an historic battle at a much later date.

After the War of 1812, while still a lieutenant in the army, Houston was asked by the governor of Tennessee to help his Cherokee friends. Sam went with the Cherokee leaders to Washington, where the Secretary of War, John C. Calhoun, gave them promises but little else. Nevertheless, his manner was so polite and friendly the Indians left with great hope for the future.

As soon as the Indian leaders had left the conference, Calhoun's manner changed. He sternly lectured Houston for dressing like his Indian friends. He was wearing an Indian-style turban around his head, with a blanket over his shoulders.

Houston replied that as a diplomat he thought he should dress like the Indians to help them keep their confidence in themselves, and he stalked out of the secretary's office.

SAM HOUSTON
IN CHEROKEE INDIAN COSTUME
From a Miniature

Preceding pages, The Battle of Tohopeka (Horseshoe Bend) has been recreated in this museum diorama; the Indians suffered a critical defeat there. Above, Sam Houston often dressed as an Indian when in the nation's capital in order to show his sympathy for their cause.

Calhoun was not only Secretary of the Army; he was also in charge of Indian affairs for the federal government. Sam was so disgusted with the secretary's dealings with the Indians that he resigned from the army, with the rank of lieutenant.

Looking for another way to make his fortune, Sam decided to become a lawyer. Law students were supposed to take an eighteen-month course, but Sam passed the examination after only six months of study. While studying, he joined a drama club. From that time on he was said to be "...a born actor; the world was his stage."

His former commander, General Andrew Jackson, had become a national hero in tribute to his wartime victories. Jackson and his wife were very fond of the young ex-lieutenant. Sam visited them often at their beautiful home called the Hermitage, near Nashville the capital of Tennessee.

From the Jacksons, Sam learned much about their hope for a great America of the future. Together, they all dreamed of new states being added to the Union until the country stretched from coast to coast. It is very likely that they talked about the prospect of Texas joining the American states, although Mexico was still a Spanish territory, and Texas was a part of it.

Sam opened his first law office in Lebanon, only about thirty miles from Nashville. He knew the value of making an impression, so he dressed as he thought a successful lawyer should. He was the very picture of success.

This appearance helped him when he went into politics. His brilliant manner of speaking (Some said this was just acting.) brought people to hear him whenever he campaigned for office. He was elected to several minor offices in Tennessee.

Then his friend Andrew Jackson suggested that he run for Congress, and Sam jumped into the campaign. He used his great command of public speaking to impress his audiences.

The people loved to hear him talk, and he sometimes went on for hours. Of course, in those days there were not so many other attractions, and listening to politicians gave the people much of the news that they could get in no other way. Sam knew how to pull out all the stops, until his oratory electrified the people.

Houston was elected and went to the House of Representatives in 1823. Before the congressional session opened, Sam visited the hall where the house was to meet. There he vowed he would do all he could to revenge the earlier insult of John C. Calhoun, who was now a senator. He spoke out against Calhoun whenever he could, but apparently did not make much headway in that campaign. This was one of the few times when he did not make good on one of his promises to himself.

Sam was much more successful in helping his old friend Andrew Jackson become president. Jackson almost made it in 1824. The election was so close it had to be decided by the House of Repre-

This portrait by I. Wood shows the young Sam Houston at the age of twenty-six, about the time he was a member of the U.S. House of Representatives.

*The friendship between Sam Houston and Andrew Jackson
began when the young Houston served under Jackson in the
War of 1812. They remained close friends until Jackson's
death. The friendship proved a rewarding one for both men.
This portrait of Jackson is attributed to Thomas Sully.*

sentatives. Unfortunately for Jackson, the house chose John Quincy Adams.

With Jackson's help, Samuel Houston was elected to his second term in congress. There again, also, he could help his friend Jackson work toward the presidential election of 1828. Although Jackson was a national hero, he also had many enemies. His foes said he wanted to be a dictator, and they blamed him for many of the country's troubles.

Jackson's supporters also attracted enemies for helping the great hero. In a letter Sam declared that his friendship to Jackson "caused me all the enemies I have." Nevertheless, he never gave up "in the firmness of my attachment."

That firmness was to bring Houston to a difficult decision. William A White wanted to become the U.S. postmaster at Nashville, Tennessee. Secretary of State Henry Clay supported White, and Jackson opposed him. Jackson wrote to Sam saying, "Attend to this," meaning see to it that White was not chosen.

Sam did everything he could to discourage White's candidacy. He even remarked that White was "not a man of upright character." When he heard about this statement, White challenged Houston to a duel. White said he must do this to defend his honor. Sam did not want to fight a duel, but he could not be considered a coward.

Chapter Four

DUELING AND DISASTER

Dueling had been popular in Europe for centuries. Men felt that they had to fight with pistols or swords every time anyone made an unpleasant or untrue comment about them, their families or friends. By Sam Houston's time dueling had been made illegal in most states, but it was still carried on in secret.

Because of his quick temper, Andrew Jackson had taken part in many duels. In fact he had even killed a man for offending his wife. Jackson took over the task of training Sam for his duel. He instructed Sam to bite on a bullet while taking aim. This would help him to shoot straight.

The lessons must indeed have helped. Sam shot his opponent in the groin and was not wounded himself. Fortunately, White recovered, much to Sam's relief.

The duel had done nothing to harm Sam's popularity. He decided to run for governor of Tennessee. He enjoyed the difficult life of campaigning. There was hardly a barn raising or a barbecue cookout that he missed in traveling all over the state. He loved to talk on and on, and people loved to hear him. His flowery oratory provided great entertainment, and people believed what he said.

On election day, Samuel Houston dressed in his best outfit, wearing a colorful Indian shirt and carelessly tossing a blanket over his shoulder. On his handsome grey stallion, he visited almost every polling place; he doffed his black beaver hat to the ladies and greeted the men cheerfully. He felt that his election as governor was almost certain. As usual, he was right, and he took over the governor's chair.

By the time Jackson became president in 1829, he and Houston had become two of the best-known men in the country. As Jackson's protege, Sam surely must have felt that the great man might be grooming him to take over when he left the presidency.

However, Sam had not yet married. His friends told him that a wife would be very helpful to a rising politician.

Sam had known Eliza Allen of Gallatin, Tennessee, since she was a little girl. The members of this very important family had long considered him a great friend. Visiting Gallatin after a long absence, Sam found that Eliza was no longer the little girl he always teased but instead was a very charming woman, eighteen years of age.

Sam said that he fell in love with her almost at once. He asked her to marry him. Eliza, however, was not so sure that she would be happy with a thirty-five-year-old man. Finally, though, she gave in to Sam and the urging of her family. They were to be married on January 22, 1829.

On his way to be married, Sam saw a raven die on the road. Since a raven was his symbol, he felt strongly that this might mean bad luck. But he went ahead with the very elaborate ceremony.

Scarcely three months after the wedding, Houston came home from a long trip, expecting a loving welcome. No one has ever known exactly what happened. Sam himself swore never to tell anything that would damage a lady's reputation, and he kept his word. He never spoke again about what had happened.

Nevertheless, he did write a letter of apology to Eliza's family saying that Eliza had been "cold" to him. Apparently he had become angry about this, and they had quarreled. In spite of this apology, Eliza went back to her family.

The mystery about this separation and eventual divorce caused all kinds of rumors to go around. People thought there must have been some dark secret, so terrible that no one could even talk about it. The rumors and the talk became so bad that Sam felt he could not continue as governor, so he resigned. He had not been a very religious man. But in order to help him in his time of trouble, he asked the minister who had married him to baptize him and admit him to the church.

Instead, the minister refused, saying the church could not accept a man of Sam's reputation. This was the last straw. Sam, the Raven Houston, decided to give up "civilization" and go to join his friends the Cherokee Indians.

Taking a river steamboat west, he was so depressed, the story is told, that he was ready to jump overboard and commit suicide. However, just at that moment a mighty eagle swooped by. Houston took this as a sign that "...a great destiny waited for me in the west." His spirits lifted somewhat, and the eagle became his symbol instead of the raven.

On the road Sam met another traveler who said he was escaping from civilization. Drinking heavily before a campfire they had made, the two decided that they were still too civilized. They took off all their clothes and threw them in the fire. Fortunately, they both had a change of clothes when they more soberly continued the journey the next morning.

When Sam reached the Indian homeland, his adoptive father, Oo-loo-te-ka, welcomed him to the home in Oklahoma where the Cherokee had been forced to move. The kindly chief said, "My wig-

When Sam returned to the Indians, Chief Oo-Loo-Te-Ka made a notable speech: "My son, eleven winters have passed since we met...and I heard you were a great chief among your people....I have heard that a dark cloud had fallen on the white path you were walking, and when it fell in your way you turned your thoughts to my wigwam. I am glad of it....We are in trouble, and the Great Spirit has sent you to us to give us council, and take trouble away from us..."

wam is yours—my home is yours—my people are yours—rest with us."

Once again Sam took on Indian customs and ways. He dressed in a fine doeskin shirt, trimmed with beads. Wearing yellow leggings and wearing his hair in a long queue added to his Indian appearance. He even said he would speak English only when it was absolutely necessary.

Swearing to do everything he could to help the Indians, Sam traveled from tribe to tribe. It appeared that he hoped to bring all the Indians together in one great confederation of the west. The Indians had been terribly treated by the U.S. government. Nevertheless, they could not agree among themselves.

In spite of their differences, Sam did manage to get the Osage, Creeks and Cherokee to sign a treaty, for the first time in thirty years. In total, Sam was responsible for more Indian treaties than any other person in U.S. history.

Of course, people to the east were suspicious. What could he be up to? Was he trying to create some kind of Indian nation in the almost empty lands to the west? Perhaps he even planned to lead an Indian army into Spanish Texas or even try to conquer Mexico itself.

Probably Sam himself did not have any very clear idea of where all this activity among the Indians might lead him. Seeking to escape from the sorrow and shame of his separation from Eliza, he had taken to drinking heavily. In fact, he became known in Cherokee as Oo-tse-tee Ar-dee-tah-skee. This means big drunk in Cherokee.

Then surprisingly he took another wife, even though he had not been divorced from Eliza, his first wife. Cherokee law permitted more than one wife, and Sam was living under that law. His bride was a beautiful and famous widow, Tiana Rogers, a niece of Chief Jolly.

Sam opened a trading post on the Neosho River and called it Wigwam Neosho. Many drinking parties continued at the Wigwam.

In spite of all Sam's work for the Indians, he could not win a seat on the Cherokee tribal council. Disturbed by this and perhaps befuddled by drink, he returned to Tennessee. There he tried to get into politics, but no one would take this drunken disgraced politician seriously.

While still in Tennessee, he persuaded a well known artist to do his portrait. But this was no ordinary portrait. Sam posed as his old Roman hero Caius Marius, dressed in a toga, standing before painted Roman columns. Perhaps in his drunken way he was trying to prove to himself that like Marius he could make a comeback. This he did, indeed, in one of history's most surprising comebacks.

On the death of his mother, Sam seemed to change. He gave up drinking and went to Washington to lobby for the Cherokee as their ambassador.

Soon after he had returned to Washington, Congressman William Stansbury declared that a man of Houston's reputation could not be trusted. Sam was so enraged by this that he challenged Stansbury to a duel. When Stansbury refused to duel, Sam sought him out and whipped him with his cane. Stansbury fought back and pulled the trigger of the gun he was carrying. Fortunately for Sam and for future history, the weapon refused to fire.

For this attack on one of its members, the House of Representatives brought him to trial in the house itself, where he had once been an honored member.

To defend himself Sam had engaged famed lawyer Francis Scott Key, best known today as the author of the *Star Spangled Banner*. Despite his great reputation, Key did not do very well at the start of the trial. Andrew Jackson was worried that Sam's troubles would harm Jackson's own political career, which had reached a critical point. Jackson's enemies were all lined up against Samuel Houston.

Sam was still wearing his Indian clothes. These, said Jackson, were too much a reminder of the past, which he felt Sam should now put behind him. He handed Sam a large sum of money and persuaded him to buy some of the finest new clothes so that he could make a better appearance at the trial.

Sam has left a description of the wardrobe he

Returning to Washington as the Cherokee ambassador, Houston was insulted by Representative William Stansbury, who refused Houston's challenge to a duel. Sam sought him out and struck him with a cane. Stansbury drew a pistol and pulled the trigger, but it misfired. Then Stansbury brought Sam to trial before the U.S. House of Representatives, and he regained his fame.

bought: "a coat of the finest material reaching to my knees, trousers in harmony of color and latest style sporting a white satin vest to match."

Perhaps even more important to the trial than the new clothes, Key became sick. This permitted Houston to present his own defense. His oratory "made history." The trial went on for more than a month, and Washington talked about little else.

The notorious Samuel Houston had made such a favorable impression on most of the members of Congress that he was let off with only a mild reprimand. The Speaker of the House remarked mildly, "I do reprimand you, accordingly," and that was that.

The trial had made Sam even more famous than he had been when he was at the peak of his earlier career. This has been called one of the most remarkable comebacks in history. Sam still remembered his historical friend Caius Marius of the remarkable Roman comeback.

"I was dying out, and had they taken me before a justice of the peace and fined me ten dollars, it would have killed me. But they gave me a national tribunal for a theatre, and that set me up again." At last he seemed able to forget about the past and look toward the future. He gave away his wedding ring from Eliza which he had always carried and made plans for a new career.

In this he had the counsel and encouragement of the new President of the United States, his old and dear friend Andrew Jackson. He and Sam spent quite a bit of time together in the White House. Although no one knows for certain, some experts feel that the two men hoped to make Texas a part of the United States. Perhaps they discussed means of acquiring Texas from Spain, which ruled all of Mexico, including Texas. If so, they may have considered trying to purchase Texas from Spain. More likely they may have talked about means of taking it away by force.

Chapter Five

ON TO TEXAS!

Sam had already made inquiries about buying land in Texas. Worried about the great numbers of American who were coming into Texas, Mexico had closed Texas to immigration. Now it had been reopened to those who would agree to become Mexican citizens. Sam, it would seem, planned to become a citizen of Mexico. When a friend gave him a razor, Houston said, "...if I have luck, this razor may some day shave the chin of the president of a republic" [Texas]. This was his way of making known his ambitions for the land of Texas and for himself as its leader.

Back in Cherokee country, Sam prepared to leave for Texas. He gave his lands and property to Tiana. When he crossed the Red River into Texas, he noted that an eagle soared above him. He took this sighting of his good luck symbol as a sign of future success in Texas.

Not long after arriving in Texas, Sam wrote to Andrew Jackson that this land he was adopting was "...the finest country to its extent in the globe."

He traveled over much of the Texas area in 1832 and 1833, covering more than 500 miles of this western region. Impetuous Sam hoped that President Jackson would take steps immediately to acquire Texas for the U.S.

However, the president was much too busy for that. Sam's old enemy John C. Calhoun of South Carolina had introduced a bill into the Senate which said that any state could withdraw from the Union if it did not agree with the acts of that Union. This was called the Doctrine of Nullification. Calhoun finally cancelled this threat, but Jackson knew the country was in no condition to take on the problems of Texas.

Meanwhile, Sam had selected land near the Trinity River. He settled there and set up a law practice among the Americans who already were living in the region. In addition to becoming Mexican citizens, all Texas residents from America had to join the Catholic church and add the name of a saint to their names. Sam Houston did all this, calling himself Paul Sam Houston.

Of course, true to his ideals about appearance, he bought new Texas style clothes, including the fanciest kind of poncho, decorated with fine embroidery. Even his horse was fancy. Sam bought a new saddle, decorated with silver fittings. On horseback Sam appeared to be "one of the most magnificent specimens of physical manhood," as one observer put it.

Sam Houston loved to dress up for every occasion, fine Indian costumes to represent his Indian friends, elegant finery for his profession and social occasions and the finest western outfits when he became a westerner. The U.S. issued this five cent Houston stamp showing him in his western finery.

37

Chapter Six

AMERICANS IN TEXAS

In one way or another, Americans had been in Texas for a good many years. Augustus Magee, an ex U.S. Army officer, had tried to conquer Texas. He gathered a volunteer group called the Republican Army of the North, with a green flag as their symbol. They had unusual success, capturing Nacogdoches, Goliad and the capital, San Antonio, in 1812. Then Magee died; Mexican forces captured most of his "army," and that was that.

Another strange turn in Texas history occurred when the notorious pirate, Jean Lafitte, sailed into Galveston Bay in 1817 and set up his pirate headquarters there. He ruled this pirate kingdom like a monarch, but U.S. forces finally drove him out.

Still another attempt to conquer Texas was

made by a Dr. James Long. He was captured and taken to Mexico City. However, the Mexicans had just overthrown the rule of Spain; they welcomed Dr. Long as a hero for fighting Spanish forces, but he was assassinated before he could return to Texas.

Moses Austin, an American, did not want to conquer Texas. Instead he wanted to lead a group of Americans to settle in Texas. At this time Texas was still controlled by Spain. Austin made a long hard trip to San Antonio to get permission of the Spanish governor to settle in Texas.

His son, Stephen Austin, wrote about this trip: "My father, after a fatiguing journey on horseback of more than 800 miles, reached Bexar (San Antonio) in November. His reception by the Governor was discouraging....The Governor not only refused to read the papers my father presented as evidence of his having formerly been a Spanish subject in Louisiana, but...ordered that he leave Texas immediately.

"In crossing the public square he accidentally met the Baron de Bastrop. They had seen each other once before in the United States....His influence with the Government was considerable....In the Baron's dwelling the object of my father's visit to the Capital of Texas was explained....The benefits that would accrue from the contemplated colony were apparent to Baron de Bastrop at the very first view.

"As my father was really unwell...a suspension of the order for his immediate departure was obtained. And at the end of a week, the permission was granted to introduce and settle three hundred families from the United States of America at any point in Texas which my father might select.

"Thus a mere accident had prevented the total failure of the preliminary step....The hardships and privations of my father's return were so severe that he was taken with fever and confined to his bed for three weeks."

Moses Austin died in 1821, but his son Stephen kept his promise to his father and brought 300 Americans to settle on the Colorado River; they called that settlement Columbus-on-the-Colorado. They also made another settlement on the Brazos River, called Washington-on-the-Brazos.

Meanwhile, in 1821, Mexico had become independent of Spain. With this change in authority, the grant to Moses Austin was no longer in effect. So Stephen Austin had to make the tiresome overland trip to Mexico City to get the new government's permission to settle.

Under Austin's good management the colonies grew and prospered. Austin was careful in selecting colonists of good character. These determined and capable people soon built homes, cultivated farms and arranged for forces to protect their land from the Indians.

The Austin settlements did not have to report

Stephen Austin, shown in this portrait by Robert Joy, is considered to be the founder of present Texas. Austin brought the first authorized U.S. citizens to what is now Texas, after his father, Moses Austin, had gained permission but died before this could be accomplished. For Sam Houston's later services, he is generally known as the Father of Texas.

to the local government of Mexico. For the first years, the Mexicans treated the Americans with great consideration. They were not required to pay taxes for five years, and past debts were forgiven.

In many ways, they enjoyed life, and Sam Houston entered into the activities of the area. The people had to create their own entertainment, and weddings were perhaps the most "entertaining" of all. Noah Smithwick wrote about one of those weddings in 1828: "When young folks danced in those days, they danced....They shuffled and double-shuffled, wired and cut the pigeons's wing, making the splinters fly....The fiddle being rather too weak to make itself heard above the din of clattering feet, we had in another fellow a clevis and pin to strengthen the orchestra, and we had a most enjoyable time."

Those enjoyments were about to fade, however. Other American leaders had come to Texas and founded other colonies. Finally the Mexican government became alarmed. Were the Americans becoming so powerful they would take over?

In 1830 they closed Texas to further American settlement and tried to shut off trade between the U.S. and Texas. Although the individual American communities had their own organization, they did not have any general control of the area. Jury trials, bail and other rights were denied them. Mexican forces and Americans began to clash.

Conditions became even worse when the Mexican leader Antonio Lopez de Santa Ana seized control of Mexico and its possessions.

At that time most Texans hoped they could work out their problems with Santa Ana. As yet they had no intentions of trying to become independent. They sent Stephen Austin to Mexico City with a proposal that Texas become a full-fledged state of Mexico. This would give the citizens their full rights. They asked Sam Houston to draft a constitution for the proposed state.

When Austin reached Mexico City, Santa Ana was well on his way to becoming a dictator. He had no intention of giving any more freedom to Texas. Austin was thrown into jail and remained in jail for nearly a year. When he was finally released and returned to Texas in September of 1835, he told his people that the situation with Mexico was hopeless. They would have to go to war to get their rights.

To keep them in line, Santa Ana sent troops into Texas. He ordered his troops to take away all cannons and other weapons. His intention was to leave the Texans without any means to defend themselves.

A group of Texans met and formed an informal government for what they hoped would become the new state of Texas. They still were not willing to declare independence. Under their plan Texas would still be a part of Mexico. They sent representatives to Washington to ask for help.

Chapter Seven

REMEMBER THE ALAMO

They chose Austin as commander-in-chief, and he set off with a small army to capture San Antonio. Unable to capture the capital city, they laid a siege around it. With Austin away, Sam Houston was selected as the commander in chief. He once joked that they chose him because he was the only Texan with a full uniform.

The Texans finally decided to try to end the siege of San Antonio. With only 300 volunteers, Texas Colonel Ben Milam stormed the town. As they advanced, the attackers had to perform such heroic deeds as tunneling through some of the thick adobe walls and advancing in the face of enemy artillery without any artillery of their own.

Finally, and amazingly, this tiny force of Texans captured San Antonio. Mexican General Perfecto do Cos was forced to surrender in December, 1835. Terribly angry at the news of this defeat, Santa Ana set off personally with a large, well equipped army to retake Texas.

After the capture of San Antonio, Texas leader Dr. James Grant made a foolish decision. He decided to invade Mexico itself. He took with him from San Antonio the wagons, supplies, ammunition, horses and most of the other materials needed to defend the city. When Sam Houston advised against such a foolish move, he was removed from his command.

However, just before he was demoted, Houston had sent frontiersman Sam Bowie to San Antonio to tell Lieutenant Colonel William Barret Travis, the commander there, to withdraw from San Antonio to a safer position. This Travis could not do because all of his wagons and horses were away on the ill-advised invasion of Mexico.

Santa Ana reached San Antonio on February 23, 1836. His forces may have totalled as many as 6,000. Meanwhile, only 157 defenders remained in Travis' group. They were able to reach an old abandoned mission known as the Alamo. Its thick adobe walls would provide some protection from an attack. Sam Houston urged the defenders to blow up the Alamo and leave while they could.

They disregarded this call, and a messenger from Travis was able to slip out of the Alamo with a desperate plea for reinforcements. Captain Al-

David "Davy" Crockett was a nationally known figure, a former congressman from Tennessee and renowned for his prowess as a frontiersman; provoked at losing an election for Congress, he moved to Texas and became one of the heroes of the Alamo, portrait by Wm. Henry Huddle.

bert Martin mustered a force totalling 32 men from Gonzales, managed to penetrate Santa Ana's lines and reach the Alamo. This heroic little group has been named The Thirty-Two Immortals.

With less than 200 defenders, including the immortals, for thirteen days Travis was able to hold off the thousands of Mexicans storming the Alamo.

But heroism was not enough. In another desperate plea for reinforcements, Travis wrote: "The enemy has demanded a surrender at discretion, otherwise, the garrison are to be put to the sword if the fort is taken—I have answered the demand with a cannon shot, and our flag still waves proudly from the walls—I shall never surrender or retreat. I call on you in the name of liberty and patriotism to come to our aid....If this call is neglected, I am determined to sustain myself as long as possible and die like a soldier who never forgets what is due to his own honor and that of his country—victory or death. William Barret Travis."

Sam Houston could hardly call his forces an army. He knew they were in no position to challenge Santa Ana at the Alamo. His commanders and the civilian authorities disagreed with him. Sometimes they even cancelled his orders. Sam knew that they needed more time to organize, but the hotheads wanted to charge in at once. When he would not do this, they let Sam go and chose another commander.

Meanwhile, with the siege of the Alamo in its last days, a convention at Washington-on-the-Brazos had drawn up a new constitution which declared Texas to be independent. Sam Houston was there, and he signed the new constitution on the second of March, which was his 43rd birthday. He wrote his name in such a way that the letter S in Sam looked like an I. The signature appeared to read "I am Houston." Once more the delegates selected Houston as Commander in Chief.

Although he knew rescue was impossible with his straggly group of volunteers, Houston set out to rescue the Alamo. Approaching San Antonio, Houston tried an old Indian trick. He put his ear to the ground. There was no rumbling of guns or cannon. He was certain that San Antonio had been captured by Santa Ana.

Soon a woman with a baby and a servant hurried in from San Antonio with news that the Alamo had fallen. All the defenders had been killed. Santa Ana had piled the bodies outside the Alamo and set them on fire.

Another Texas town, Goliad, was defended by 300 more Texans. Houston ordered James W. Fan-

Previous pages, "Dawn at the Alamo." This famous painting by H. A. Mc Ardle depicts the scene of the conflict, which was to end with the massacre of all the defenders, giving rise to the cry "Remember the Alamo," one of the great battle cries of all time.

nin, the commander there, to retreat while he could. Fannin evacuated Goliad with his tiny army. He was forced to surrender nearby. Santa Ana had promised them honorable terms. The treacherous Mexican general went back on his word and ordered the entire group massacred.

However, turning against her own soldiers, Senora Alvarez, wife of one of the Mexican officers, managed to help twenty-seven of the prisoners to escape. Ever since that time, Senora Alvarez has been known as the Angel of Goliad. The news of these senseless slaughters so enraged the Americans that they wanted to march at once against Santa Ana. About 1,600 volunteers were in training under Houston, but they still knew little about fighting. As Santa Ana advanced, many of the volunteers deserted and went back to defend their homes and families.

Instead of foolishly hurling his force at the Mexican hordes, Houston began to retreat. He knew that his little, poorly trained group could never stand against the 6,000 trained soldiers of Mexico.

His opponents said he did not know what he was doing, and some even called him a coward. Yet for forty days Houston continued to move his troops east through heavy rains toward the coast of the Gulf of Mexico. In this retreat he continued to outfox Santa Ana. Houston wrote, "My policy was to concentrate, retreat, and conquer." Reaching

Preparing to battle Santa Ana, at last, Houston spent the evening working out the details and dictating letters and memos, as shown in this illustration entitled "Houston Dictating Orders to Adjutant Hockley."

the Gulf, he hoped other Americans would come in from the east to help them.

At Buffalo Bayou, the Texans could find no way of getting their ammunition across this body of water. Finally Sam ordered them to tear down the nearby house belonging to Isaac Batterson. This gave them enough lumber to make a raft to ferry the ammunition across to San Jacinto where they made camp in a grove of live oak trees on a bluff above the San Jacinto River.

From this height the Texans could watch the armies of Santa Ana working their way across the plains. Describing the situation, Houston wrote: "This morning we are in preparation to meet Santa Ana. It is the only chance of saving Texas. From time to time I have looked for reinforcements in vain....Texas could have started at least four thousand men. We will only have about seven hundred to march with....We go to conquer..."

Meanwhile, the rain had caused Santa Ana's troops to separate. The dictator himself was leading a small group of only about 1,500 men eastward, following the Texans. He made camp near Buffalo Bayou on San Jacinto Bay.

The Texans could retreat no further. They must fight. Selecting this site was part of Sam Houston's well-made plans. However, he would not let anyone in on his secrets. He slept late on the morning of April 21. When he finally awoke and looked up, he saw an eagle circling in the sky. Good luck, he thought to himself.

Time went by. The Texas soldiers could not understand what Sam was waiting for. But Houston knew that Mexicans always take an afternoon nap, or siesta. He hoped they would do the same that afternoon. At three o'clock, he finally tapped on his drum, called his men together and formed his troops. At four, he jumped on his white stallion and lifted his sword. The only battle music came from a fife and drum. The ragtag soldiers marched swiftly. They did not know any battle songs, so they sang the latest love song of the day: "Will You come to the Bower I have shaded for you?"

Chapter Eight

A BATTLE OF WORLD IMPORTANCE

The Mexicans were taken completely by surprise. Shouting "Remember the Alamo! Remember Goliad!" the Americans poured rifle fire into the astonished Mexicans. The Texans had two cannons which had been given to them by the people of Ohio. They called these the Twin Sisters.

They had no cannon balls for the twins, so they filled them with horseshoes and bombarded the foes with horseshoes. They went into hand-to-hand combat with Bowie knives.

Houston had planned his attack so that the western sun would be in the enemy eyes. The Texans had destroyed the escape bridges. The Mexicans could not escape through the marshes, which were full of rainwater. In less than twenty minutes, the remaining enemy forces surrendered.

Once again Sam Houston was wounded, this time leading his army to victory at San Jacinto. His horse was shot out from under him, and he was wounded in the leg, but he rose up, took another horse and continued to direct the battle, while his boot filled with blood.

Six-hundred-thirty Mexicans had been killed, 208 wounded and 730 taken prisoner. Texas had lost nine men.

Once again, however, Sam Houston had been wounded in battle, this time in the leg. His horse had been shot from under him. He seized another horse, and that also was shot. Although his boot was filling with blood, Houston fought until the battle ended.

That night the Texans celebrated. Next day they all had a great and pleasant surprise. The last man to be captured was dressed like a common soldier. However, when the other prisoners saw him they drew back in awe and murmured "El Presidente!" This disguised man was Santa Ana himself. The fierce Mexican leader was one of the captives.

Sam Houston was lying under an oak tree while the doctor worked to dress his wound. Santa Ana was brought before him. The dictator asked for his freedom, calling out: "That man may consider himself born to no mean future who has vanquished the Napoleon of the West. Now it remains for him to be generous to the vanquished."

"What right have you to plead for mercy when you showed none at the Alamo?" Houston roared back.

"I had orders taken from my government to execute all prisoners bearing arms."

"You were the government. A dictator has no

superior. Your butchery at the Alamo and Goliad has no equal for cruelty, and it cannot be justified under any pretext!"

The Texas soldiers drew closer. Some murmured that the dictator should be lynched at once. The dictator shivered.

Houston spoke again: "You must write an order at once demanding that all your troops in Texas leave the state forthwith, returning to Mexico."

"This I will do immediately," the dictator responded meekly, to save his life.

The Texans held the upper hand. They kept Santa Ana hostage until their demands were met. A free Republic of Texas was assured.

This small battle of San Jacinto looms large in history. Many experts call it one of the ten major battles of world history—a battle from which great changes resulted. The victory had come about as the result of Houston's courage, planning and bravery.

And so, as the winning general, Sam Houston earned his place among the great world generals. His determination and careful reasoning resulted in a great victory. He was hailed as "The Hero of San Jacinto." Of all the many nicknames given him during his lifetime, Sam Houston said the one he liked the best was that one. Yet some of the most important events of Sam Houston's life were just beginning.

The famed painting by William Henry Huddle shows Mexican Dictator Santa Ana pieading for his life before the wounded Sam Houston who was resting under a tree while his wounds were cared for.

Chapter Nine

AN INDEPENDENT REPUBLIC

Once again Sam had to go to New Orleans for medical attention. His wound had become infected. Again he was near death. At New Orleans the surgeon lifted twenty splinters of bone from his leg. Strangely, the surgeon was the same one who had treated his old wound from the Battle of Horseshoe Bend. Samuel Houston never completely recovered from this later wound. He limped badly and suffered much constant pain.

But his heroism had more positive results. The people elected him president of the new Republic of Texas. Dressed in velvet and lace and wearing a crimson vest, he was inaugurated on October 22, 1836. In his inaugural address he spoke of his hopes for the new nation.

He expected the world to respect and recog-

Photograph of Houston at about the time of his inauguration on October 22, 1836, when he became the first President of the newly founded Republic of Texas. This portrait shows few of the lines and worries brought on by the cares of office, which are so evident in photographs made only a few years later.

nize this new country of more than 65,000 people. The new republic would be governed along the same democratic lines on which the U.S. had been founded, and would be carried on in the manner of Washington, Jefferson and Jackson.

The new capital of the republic had been named Houston in his honor. Although the president's house was then a two-room log cabin, Sam predicted that some day Houston would become a great city. That prediction has certainly come true.

Nevertheless, the new Republic of Texas was off to a shaky start. There was no money to run a government. Conditions were uncertain during most of Houston's first term as president. However, Houston's good management brought gradual improvement. He established courts and a system of justice, managed to pay official salaries, to deliver mail and erect a small capitol with square pillars in front.

Still few Texans thought the country could survive alone. Most felt it must be joined to the United States. On the first anniversary of independence a group gathered, and a toast to annexation was proposed. The toast was given to "Uncle Sam's big cornfield and his son Sam's cotton patch—may they soon be united in one big plantation."

Annexation was still a long way off, but Andrew Jackson did the best he could. The day following the toast, March 3, 1837, U.S. President

This reproduction of an antique postcard shows Sam Houston's old house in his namesake city of Houston.

Andrew Jackson gave the U.S. government's official recognition of the Republic of Texas as an independent nation. This was the last act of his administration as U.S. president.

As his term also came to a close, Houston wrote to his friend Andrew Jackson, "No man living can so well appreciate the difficulties which have beset me, as yourself....You, General, have left monuments of glory to your country....But you had an organized Government and men who were accustomed to civil rule while I had to command a Government from chaos, with men who had never been accustomed as a community to any rule, but their passions, nor to any government but their will. You had experience with mature wisdom. I lacked experience." He went on to say that he would remain loyal to the principles "which you inculcated upon me in my early life...while life lasts."

When his term expired, the Texas constitution kept Sam Houston from serving another term. This sorrowed and depressed him, but there was nothing he could do. A new president was elected.

Even worse, Houston disliked the new president, Mirabeau B. Lamar. They had had many disagreements about Sam's leadership. On Lamar's inaugural day, Houston had not even been invited to attend the ceremony. However, he came anyway, intending to steal the show, which he managed to do. He dressed as George Washington, pretending to be the father of Texas, just as Washington was the father of his country.

The crowd went mad and called for him to speak. While the new president fidgeted and sweated, Sam talked for three hours, and the crowd loved it. Lamar was so upset, he had to have his assistant read his speech.

The new leader was determined to remake Texas according to his own ideas. He would keep as little as possible to remind the Texans of their first president. Lamar selected a new capital, to be called Austin in honor of the man he said was the true father of Texas.

Lamar was against making Texas a part of the U.S. Why downgrade a great new nation to a state among other states?

To keep from watching Lamar ruin Texas, as he thought, Sam left his beloved country in the spring of 1839 and went back to visit Andrew Jackson in the Hermitage.

Returning to Texas, he stopped to visit at the plantation of William Bledsoe in Alabama. There he was invited to attend a strawberry festival where he met Margaret Lea, the twenty-year-old sister of Mrs. Bledsoe.

From the moment the tall and beautiful Margaret Lea appeared at the festival, Sam was smitten. Although there was a difference of twenty-six years in their ages, the younger woman appeared to be equally taken with Houston.

Of all the political friendships in the national history, that between Andrew Jackson and Samuel Houston is among the most memorable. Sam spent much time at the beautiful Nashville home of Jackson, called the Hermitage, where he was comforted by Jackson when in trouble and counseled on many important political matters.

By this time, Sam was free to marry. His divorce from Eliza was final. Tiana, his second wife, was dead. He now could marry if he wished. Margaret Lea may not have said she would marry Sam during that visit, but she was eagerly looking forward to the next visit he had promised to make.

Back in Texas, Sam found that conditions were even worse than he had feared. President Lamar hated the Indians, especially Sam's friends the Cherokee. At this time the Cherokee were led by a good friend of Houston, a chief known as The Bowl. The Bowl was a striking looking man, son of a Scotch-Irish father and Cherokee mother.

The Bowl had been trying to work out a treaty with the Texas government for recognition of the boundaries of land claimed by the Cherokee. The treaty had been agreed upon but was not yet signed. President Lamar did not approve of the treaty. Nor did he approve of kindness and consideration of the Indians.

Lamar said that the white man had been kind to the Indians, but they had misued that friendship, and they could not be trusted. The Bowl did not want war, but hotheaded younger braves of his tribe insisted that fighting was the only way to solve their problems. They forced the chief to begin a war that he was sure the Indians could never win.

Nevertheless, at the age of eighty-three he led his troops into battle. He entered the fight carrying the sword given to him by Sam Houston. He made a striking figure as he rode his handsome horse.

Just as the chief had predicted, the battle was a terrible defeat for the Indians. Leading his wounded horse, The Bowl was following his defeated troops off the battlefield when one of the Texas soldiers shot him in the back. As he fell, he turned to face the Texans, and one of them shot the distinguished old leader in the head.

This treachery horrified Sam Houston when he came back to Texas and learned about it. In a bitter speech he thundered that his friend was a far better person and a better leader than anyone who had anything to do with his execution.

Of course, Sam Houston did not like Austin, the new capital. He had labeled it "the most unfortunate site upon earth for the Seat of Government." Naturally, he would much have preferred to have the capital at his own Houston.

Sam watched as Lamar cooked up more and more ways of running Texas into debt. One of the most costly and foolish of all of his schemes was his attempt to capture Santa Fe. Texas had long claimed the land that is now New Mexico. However, it remained firmly in Mexican control.

Lamar asked the Texas legislature to authorize an attack on Santa Fe to capture land he believed belonged to his country. Although the legislature refused, Lamar went ahead on his own. He sent a small troop of Texas soldiers to attack the town that for generations had been the capital of Spanish and Mexican interests in the entire area. As everyone had predicted, the move was a disaster. All of the more than 300 Texans were captured by the Mexicans.

About the only bright spot for Sam Houston during this time was his marriage to Margaret Lea. Her family had been against the marriage. They called Sam a drunkard. They said he was far too old for her. Not only did he never attend church, but the church would not even permit him to be baptized.

Even Sam's friends felt that the marriage would never last. They thought that he could not be happy tied down to a wife and family. In spite of all the gloomy forecasts, Sam and Margaret were married. They made their home in a summer cottage Houston had acquired at Cedar Point, overlooking Galveston Bay.

As a married man, Sam agreed to give up drinking. This may have been one of the hardest promises for him to keep. Whenever he felt like drinking, it was said that he took out a little bottle of ammonia which he always carried. A strong sniff of the ammonia helped to overcome the urge to drink.

Perhaps Margaret worried that he would not be strong enough to keep his promises when he was away from home, but apparently he was true to his word. When Sam was reelected president of Texas

This very rare daguerrotype was fortunately salvaged as the only record of Sam Houston's appearance in 1841 or 1842. Reproduced unretouched it represents photography in its very early period.

in 1841, there was no liquor at the inaugural celebration.

It was not surprising that Houston had been elected president once again. Times had become harder than ever because of the debt Lamar had built up. Because the records had not been kept properly, no one even knew exactly how much the government owed. The government could not even afford firewood for the president's house.

Times were so bad that when Sam and his family moved into that house they found that looters had taken or destroyed almost everything inside. Only three or four usable items remained.

Worst of all, however, Santa Ana was in a rage over the attack on Santa Fe and planned to retake Texas. War would make matters even more difficult. Sam felt he must put the country on a drastic program to save money. Texas did not have any funds to support an army against Mexican invasion.

Santa Ana's threats were not the only problem. Texans had learned that the soldiers who had been captured in the attempt to take Santa Fe had been tortured on their way to prison in Mexico City. Many citizens called out for revenge, even for invading Mexico.

With great effort, the president scraped together enough government funds to support a small army which managed to defend the country. The Mexicans made many raids across the border, but they failed to make any permanent gains. Houston also was able to resist the demands of the hotheads to invade Mexico. He managed to keep things on an even keel.

Perhaps Sam was still afraid that the capital would be captured. Perhaps he saw the threat of capture as a good way to force the Texas capital to move back to Houston. When he did this, howls of rage went up from the supporters of Austin, so again the capital was changed—this time to Washington-on-the-Brazos.

Houston ordered all the Texas official documents, the government archives, to be moved from Austin to Washington. The Austin people felt that if the papers were removed, Austin might never get the capital back again. They actually had a little struggle and by force kept Sam's people from moving the papers out. This little battle has gone down in Texas history as "The Archives War."

Washington was not much of a capital. The national house of representatives had to meet on the second floor over a liquor store. The senate meeting place was located over a saloon. So many house members stopped in at the bar that Houston ordered an outside stairway put in so that the members would not be tempted as they passed by the liquor.

Meanwhile, Margaret had gone back to live with her mother in Liberty County in the eastern part of the state, where she would be safe from

Mexican invasion. With Margaret gone and with all the problems of the government, Sam, himself, went back to drinking. Visiting her in January, 1843, Houston asked her to return to Washington-on-the-Brazos with him, even though she was expecting their first child.

When she agreed, Sam even hauled her rosewood piano back to Washington-on-the-Brazos. To make life a little easier, he bought a silver service, some new fancy china and some other little luxuries. Altogether, it seemed, times were getting better in Texas in 1843, thanks to the careful administration of President Houston. Indian treaties with several important tribes helped to keep the peace. The Mexicans even seemed afraid to attack again. At last the crops could be gathered in peace.

Even more important for the Houstons, was Sam, Jr., who arrived on May 25, 1843. Sam wrote, "May he never be a loafer or an agitator!"

Sam was very anxious to be seen as a president of the common man. Every morning he shaved on the back porch of the presidential "mansion." This gave the people an opportunity to talk with the president personally. They could keep him informed on their problems and let him know how they felt about his actions as chief executive.

Sam's main concern and that of many of his back porch visitors was how to get the United States to take Texas over as a state. All during the presidency of Andrew Jackson, Sam had kept after his friend to annex Texas. Next he threatened to make a treaty with England. This would put England back on the North American continent, perhaps as a danger to the United States.

Unhappily for Sam this threat had not worked, and the U.S. congress had not acted to annex Texas before Houston's term as president once more had come to a close in December, 1844. This time, however, Sam was not so distressed. His good friend, Anson Jones, was now the president of Texas. He was a good leader, and, best of all, he was just as anxious as Sam to have Texas become a U.S. state.

The major problem blocking such a move was the fear of many U.S. lawmakers that admitting Texas would bring in a new slave state to the Union. This would upset the balance of power between the slave states and the free states.

However, both retired presidents, Andrew Jackson and James K. Polk, urged outgoing President John Tyler to act on Texas' annexation. On March 1, 1845, the last act of Tyler as U.S. president was to sign a resolution calling for the Republic of Texas to become a U.S. state.

Because Houston had seemed to turn against the union when he urged closer ties with Britain, no one was sure how he stood. Although he was no longer in office, he still had great power in Texas, and the president was his friend. However, statehood had always been Sam's dream. All of his other actions had been taken to make the U.S. feel it might lose Texas if it did not take action quickly.

So when that action finally came, Sam approved. In December, 1845, the young nation gladly accepted the move to join the Union. Two months later Anson Jones lowered the Lone Star flag of Texas, and Sam Houston gathered it in his arms. The Stars and Stripes then went up over the largest state in the Union. At last Samuel Houston's fondest dream had been realized.

Now that Samuel Houston was a private citizen, his wife very much wanted him to quit public life and retire. Certainly, with all his high positions and honors he deserved retirement. But Sam Houston was too restless and ambitious to quit his life's work. He also knew that difficult times were ahead, and he wanted to be able to help his beloved Texas.

The new state elected Sam Houston as its first U.S. senator. To no one's great surprise, he accepted. He moved to Washington but left his family in Texas. Once again he was determined to be noticed. Although he generally wore conventional clothes, to get attention he might appear in a Mexican blanket and wide sombrero. Even in the Senate he wore clothing of a military style.

All of this desire to attract attention was said to be part of Houston's broader plan to become President of the United States. He once wrote to Margaret, "Were I the nation's ruler, I could rule it well."

This rare etching was made during the time when Sam Houston was a senator from the new State of Texas and shows his florid signature.

Houston had not been in Washington long when it appeared there might be a war with Mexico. Many in authority thought war could be avoided. However, Houston knew the Mexicans. He felt they would never forgive the United States for taking Texas into the Union. War with Mexico came in 1846, and Houston gave it his support.

When the bitter war ended two years later, Houston was delighted for two reasons. The fighting and bloodshed were over, and the war had brought the United States territory on the Pacific Ocean. At last, as he and Jackson had dreamed so long ago, the country they loved now stretched from coast to coast. He gave it his support.

Chapter Ten

A DIVIDED NATION

New territory meant that new states would be added. Would they be slave states or free states? This was the time when the dispute over slavery was growing ever more bitter. People of the North generally wanted to have the slaves freed. The South wanted to keep their slaves to do the hard work, to "own" them, as they had for so long.

Although Houston himself owned slaves, and he represented a slave state, he refused to take the side of the South. He was sure that the dispute over slavery could break up the country. He worked hard to find a peaceful means of settling the slavery question. He was not in favor of the radicals on either side who would do anything to win their cause.

In 1850, when Henry Clay brought out a bill to compromise between the North and South, Houston was in favor of it. When he spoke out in favor of it he said, "A nation divided against itself cannot stand." This expression was later to become famous when it was used by Abraham Lincoln. Congress passed the bill.

While he was in Washington, Sam surprised almost everyone by attending church with some regularity, although he would not join the church because he felt he was not worthy to join. During church services, he had a very unusual habit. He would whittle on a piece of wood, creating simple objects. These he would give to the children after the service. The minister must have been rather distracted as he preached while Sam whittled in the front row.

The former "Big Drunk" had stopped drinking entirely. He spoke at meetings of societies that opposed drinking. At such meetings, he made the observation that so many heavy drinkers have made: Some people could drink a small amount and not have any trouble. As for Sam Houston, he had discovered he could not drink at all.

Previous page, an 1848 lithograph depicts Houston growing older, revealing the toll taken by cares of office and country. He was still writing with a firm hand but with a more modest signature than that shown on previous page 76.

During his time in the U.S. Senate, Houston had built a new home at Huntsville, Texas. One of the most unusual features of this house was its "dogtrot." This was a hall which went from front to back through the house. The family dogs loved to dash through the open door, skidding on the slippery floor and clattering out the back.

Sam was not inclined to be very neat in some of his habits. In the main house, he had to watch out or he would do something that upset Margaret. She particularly disliked his habit of spitting into a spittoon, which he often missed. In order to have a real place of his own, Sam built a study of logs behind the house. There, whenever the senate was not in session, he could really do what he pleased, whittle and let the shavings pile up or take a long shot in the general region of the spittoon.

As the election of 1852 drew near, Sam was talked up as a candidate for president. He was in great demand as a speaker, but he did not call himself a candidate. Houston for President clubs were organized, and there were other indications that he might run. At the nominating convention, Sam was nominated. However, there were so many presidential hopefuls that the convention could not decide.

Sam withdrew his name and threw his support to Franklin Pierce. On the 49th ballot, Pierce won the nomination.

During the remainder of Houston's time in the

While Houston was in the U.S. Senate he built his "dogtrot" house at Huntsville Texas. This type of house, with a large open central hall down the middle, was very popular in the South at the time. The household dogs and other pets loved to dash into the house, through the hall and out of the house at the opposite end.

Senate it became more and more difficult to find a way to admit new states to the Union. If a proposed state held slaves, the North opposed it. If the state were to be free, with no slaves, of course the South was against having it admitted.

This was particularly true of Kansas and Nebraska. Congress had been putting off organizing this area into territories. Finally, Illinois Senator Stephen A. Douglas introduced a compromise. The settlers of Kansas and Nebraska would be permitted to decide whether or not they would own slaves.

Sam Houston could foresee, perhaps more clearly than anyone else, what would happen if this bill passed. Those who were against slavery would do everything they could to get opponents of slavery to settle in the territories. The southern block would do everything it could to prevent free settlement. Houston predicted that there would be struggles and death in the territories, perhaps even leading to civil war.

After the Kansas-Nebraska Act passed in 1854, everything Sam Houston had predicted did come about, and more.

During his twelve years in the U.S. Senate, Samuel Houston was always one of the principal defenders of the federal government. He opposed any talk of weakening it or breaking it up. This position caused his fellow southerners to feel he was a traitor to their cause. His fight against the

Kansas-Nebraska Act was the last straw. Many said he would never again hold any public office.

In spite of this, Sam Houston called his vote against the Kansas-Nebraska Act the "wisest and most patriotic" think he had ever done. "Because the entire south is wrong, should I be wrong too?"

Back in Texas, Sam and his family made still another move, this time to a house they had built in Independence, Texas. There he finally came to terms with a religious matter that had been bothering him almost all of his life. After hearing a particularly moving sermon, Sam Houston decided to be baptized and join the church.

The night before Sam and nineteen others were to be immersed in the baptismal font, some pranksters filled the font with debris. The converts had to be taken to nearby Rocky Creek. The minister and the converts were all dressed in long white robes. Someone has said, "What a shame television had not been invented, the great Sam Houston in a white robe. What a spectacle today's television would have made of that!"

As for Sam himself, he kept his composure and his wit. When a friend slyly commented that "Now your sins have been washed away," Sam replied, "But if they are all washed away, the Lord help those fish down there."

In 1857 Texas began to look toward the election of a governor. Hardin Runnels became a candidate. Runnels stood for everything Sam opposed, and he said he was running on an anti-Houston platform. This was too much for Sam; he too became a candidate. He made a whirlwind campaign trip in a fancy buggy, and stirred up great excitement wherever he went.

And he certainly did go! He covered 1,550 miles by buggy. He spoke to forty-seven different audiences, sometimes going on for four hours without a stop.

After all this, he was defeated.

Nevertheless, Sam ran for governor of Texas in 1859 and won. Among the other reasons for his success, the people now realized that he had been absolutely right about the Kansas-Nebraska Act.

In contrast to the modest homes which were all the state could provide in earlier times, now the governor and his family were living in a splendid new governor's mansion at Austin.

Even this large new house was crowded by the family Sam had gathered around him. Now there were seven children, and another was born later. Many stories are told about the pranks pulled by the Houston boys.

As an example, one of the boys—Andrew Jackson Houston— locked the entire Texas state senate in its meeting room and hid the key. He refused to give the key back. In fact, he would not give in until his father threatened to send him to jail. So he finally unlocked the door and released a group of angry senators.

During this period Sam enjoyed his family. But almost everything else was going wrong. He could see that conditions in the country were growing rapidly worse. The people of the North were determined to wipe out slavery. The people of the South were determined to keep it. They claimed it was right to "own" black people and control their lives.

Southern politicians claimed that the states could leave the union, or secede, if they could not agree with the national government. They said they had a right to form a new nation of states which held slaves.

Splitting up the United States was the one thing Houston feared most. He did everything he could to keep the nation together. He spoke out against those who thought the states had a right to leave the union. He called for people of good will on both sides to remember they were really brothers and sisters with a common cause.

Was there anything he could do to help matters? Perhaps even at this late date he could run for president. Moderate people on both sides knew how Sam felt about keeping the United States together. It was just possible he could still do it, if they would only elect him. One supporter in New England pointed out that, "He has his peculiarities, but the people have faith in 'Old Sam.'"

A group of his followers gathered on the San Jacinto battlefield and nominated Houston for

Temple Lea Houston was the fourth son and youngest child of the Houstons. Lea was his mother's family name. He made a reputation of his own as a gun-toting lawyer-explorer.

president. Samuel Houston agreed to accept if he could be a national candidate, a candidate of all the people. When he made this announcement, a huge rally in New York City approved his nomination.

The actions of the Democratic Party were entirely different. Of course, the members of the party from the North and those from the South could not agree, so they broke into two groups. The northern group nominated Stephen Douglas of Illinois. The South backed J.C. Breckinridge, a Calhoun follower. Yet another party, the newly formed Constitutional Union Party, also had a candidate.

With four men running against Abraham Lincoln, Sam knew that Lincoln would be a sure winner. Samuel Houston withdrew. He wrote to a friend, "I forgot to tell you that I am out of the scrape for President. I am arms folded." He must have known that his worst fears about the nation were about to be realized.

His withdrawal did not mend the split in the Democratic Party. Abraham Lincoln won the most votes of the divided nation and became president. Still Sam appealed for calm and reason. "The Union is worth more than Mr. Lincoln. Wait and see."

All of this came when Sam was having a difficult time at home. Margaret had become very ill with the birth of their fourth son and last child, Temple Lea, when she was forty-one years of age.

During this time, Sam scarcely left her side.

One by one the southern states began to leave the union. They set up a new government called the Confederate States of America. The "new nation" urged all the other states of the South to secede from the union and join the Confederacy.

As usual, Sam Houston wanted to hold the United States together. But this time things had gone so far that he could not help. Most Texans now thought he was an enemy of the state he had founded and always had loved so much. Rocks were thrown at him. Some who hated him the most even threatened to kill him.

"Let me tell you what is coming," Houston warned. "Your fathers and husbands, your sons and brothers, will be herded at the point of a bayonet. You may, after the sacrifice of countless millions, win southern independence...but I doubt it."

No one could have been a better prophet!

Chapter Eleven

LEAVE HIM TO HISTORY

The people of Texas were asked to vote: Should Texas join the Confederacy? Only eighteen counties voted to stay in the Union. One hundred and four counties voted to pull out. The Texas legislature was not even permitted to vote.

Instead, an anti-Union convention voted to join the Confederate States. Of course, Governor Houston said this was not legal. But no one listened. The convention insisted that all state officers must swear to be loyal to the new Confederate nation.

When the state officials gathered to take the required loyalty oath, Governor Sam Houston was not there. They called his name three times, but he had decided to give up his position as governor. He could not take an oath to break up the union. The next morning "Little Eddie" Clark was sitting in Sam Houston's chair in the governor's office. Clark was sworn in to replace Houston as governor.

Soon after this, Houston made another warning speech: "I protest against surrendering the Federal Constitution, its government and its glorious flag to...a so-called Confederate Government whose constitution contains the germs and seeds of decay which must and will lead to its speedy ruin....The soil of our beloved South will drink deep the precious blood of our sons and brethren....You must before long reap the fearful harvest of conspiracy and revolution."

Certainly, Sam Houston was right about the terrible cost of war. Hundreds of thousands died unnecessarily. The entire nation—both North and South—suffered untold hardships during the war. When the war came to an end the South had been almost destroyed.

When he was forced out of the governor's chair, Houston was hated by many people in both the South and North. His southern neighbors thought he was a traitor to their cause. Most northerners disliked him because they thought he was too loyal to the South.

Over the years, of course, both Sam Houston and the South have made comebacks, as Sam would probably be pleased to know.

"His stature has increased with time," according to a well-known writer. This writer was

Famed photographer Matthew Brady made this famous photograph of Samuel Houston in 1862. It is thought to be the last likeness of the great man.

President John F. Kennedy, who selected Houston as one of the notable Americans in his book *Profiles in Courage.*

Another famous personality, "Lady Bird" Johnson (wife of President Lyndon Johnson), also wrote about Houston: "He was one of us...courageous, so daring. Flamboyant, yes, but he was also tough and a man of vision who dreamed big dreams."

Lamar Alexander, Governor of Tennessee, named his son William Houston Alexander and described Sam Houston as "The most interesting figure in Tennessee history." He was, said Alexander, "much too large for Texas or any single state."

The great city of Houston, Texas, bears his name. Near that city is one of the world's tallest monuments. It was raised on the place where the Battle of San Jacinto was fought. This mighty shaft honors the hero of that battle. Houston's victory there assured Sam Houston of a place in history as one of the world's most successful generals.

Most Americans today have heard Sam Houston's name, but few recognize the real importance of the man who held more high public offices than any other person in U.S. history.

After Sam Houston was forced out as governor, he returned to Huntsville, Texas, and rented a house there. This house was built to look like a Mississippi River steamboat. It had the shape of a steamboat, with decks and ladders. Someone said Sam "looked like a man who, along with his boat, was anchored safely at last in his home port."

When Union troops captured Vicksburg, Mississippi, Sam Houston knew that the Confederacy would lose the war, just as he had predicted.

Soon after that, Sam Houston took pneumonia. He was seventy years old. He must have felt that he and the southern cause would go down together.

He lingered for three weeks, growing weaker every day.

On July 26, 1863, the great Samuel Houston lay dying, with his wife at his side. With his last breath he whispered, "Margaret — Texas — Texas." Even at his death his last thoughts were of his wife and the state he loved so well.

One of his friends mourned his death, saying "Leave him to history."

History is really just beginning to catch up to Samuel Houston.

In 1986 the U.S. government issued a twenty-two cent stamp to commemorate the battle of San Jacinto, with the silver spur as a symbol of the man who won that battle, Samuel Houston.

HIGHLIGHTS

1793, March 2, Samuel Houston born near Lexington, Virginia

1808, Runs away to live with Indians

1813, March 24, Joins U. S. Army

1814, March 20, Battle of Horseshoe Bend

1815, Wounds treated at New Orleans

1818, March 1, resigns from army

1823, Becomes U. S. congressman

1825, Reelected to congress

1827, Governor of Tennessee

1829. January 22, marries Eliza Allen

1829, June, resigns governorship, returns to Cherokee friends

1831, Mother's death a sobering influence; becomes ambassador of the Cherokee at Washington

1832, Leaves Washington, leaves Cherokee for Texas

1835, Stephen Austin returns to Texas from Mexico, predicts Texas will war with Mexico

1836, February 23, Santa Ana reaches San Antonio

1836, March 2, Houston signs Texas declaration of independence on 43rd birthday

1836, March 6, Alamo falls

1836, April 21, Houston triumphs in Battle of San

Jacinto; battle has world importance

1836, October 22, Houston becomes first President of Texas

1837, March 3, U.S. President Andrew Jackson recognizes Texas as an independent nation

1838, New Texas President Mirabeau Lamar takes over

1839, Houston visits Tennessee and Andrew Jackson, meets future bride

1840, Marries Margaret Lea

1841, Starts second term as Texas President, serves until 1844

1843, May 25, first child, Sam, Jr., born

1845, December 29, Congress approves Texas as a U.S. state

1846, Houston's first term in U.S. Senate, serves 12 years

1850, Supports Compromise of 1850

1852, Withdraws as U.S. presidential candidate

1857, Defeated in try for Texas governorship

1859, Opposes Kansas-Nebraska Act, elected Texas governor

1861, Deposed from governor's chair by Texas secessionists

1863, July 26, Samuel Houston is dead

Today the Alamo is a world shrine to freedom.

SOURCES OF FURTHER INFORMATION

University of Texas Press, *The Writings of Sam Houston 1813-1863*
Eight volumes, Amelia M. Williams and Eugene D. Barker, (1938-43)
University of Oklahoma Press, *The Autobiography of Sam Houston,* (1954)
Flanagan, Sue, *Sam Houston's Texas,* University of Texas Press
Biography, Friend, Llerna, University of Texas Press (1954, reprinted 1969)

SPEECH AT BRENHAM, TEXAS
March 31, 1861
By Samuel Houston

Author's Note: The following speech has been considered one of the finest made by Houston. It ranks high among all speeches dealing with secession and the rights of states and the crime and horrors of civil war.

Fellow-Citizens; It was not my purpose or desire to address you today upon the great issues now confronting our common country, but old soldier comrades who fought with me at San Jacinto, and other dear friends, insist that I explain the reason why I refuse to take the oath of allegiance to the Confederate Government, and why I have been deposed from the Governorship of our beloved State. The earnest solicitations of my old soldier comrades outweigh my desire to remain silent until the whirlwind of passion and popular clamor have subsided and the voice of reason can be fairly heard.

I shall, therefore, speak my honest sentiments and convictions and I now submit to you the reasons why I could not take the oath of allegiance to the so-called Confederate Government, and thereby violate the oath of allegiance I took to the Federal Government when I entered upon the duties of the Chief Magistracy of Texas. It has always been the invariable rule of my life never to form an opinion or verdict upon any great public question until I have first carefully and impartially heard and considered all the evidence and facts upon both sides, and when I have thus formed my verdict, no fear of popular condemnation can induce me to modify or change such verdict. I have never permitted popular clamor, passion, prejudice nor selfish ambition to induce me to change an opinion or verdict which my conscience and judgment has once formed and tells me is right. My only desire is to be right, and for this reason I can not nor will not sacrifice what my conscience and judgment tells me is right. I love the plaudits of my fellow citizens, but will never sacrifice the principle of right and justice for public favor or commendation.

The Vox Populi is not always the voice of God, for when demagogues and selfish political leaders succeed in arousing public prejudice and stilling the voice of reason, then on every hand can be heard the popular cry of "Crucify him, crucify him." The Vox Populi then becomes the voice of the devil, and the hiss of mobs warns all patriots that peace and good government are in peril. I have heard the hiss of mobs upon the streets of Austin, and also heard the hiss of mobs upon the streets of Brenham, and friends have warned me that my life was in great peril if I expressed my honest sentiments and convictions.

But the hiss of the mob and the howls of their jackal leaders can not deter me nor compel me to take the oath of allegiance to a so-called Confederate Government. I protest against surrendering the Federal Constitution, its Government and its glorious flag to the Northern abolition leaders and to accept in its stead a so-called Confederate Government whose constitution contains the germs and seeds of decay which must and will lead to its speedy ruin and dismemberment if it can ever secure any real existence. Its seeds of ruin and decay are the principle of secession which permits any one or more of the Confederate States to secede from the parent Confederate Government and to establish separate governments. Can any well-informed man doubt that the time will soon come when several of the Confederate States will secede and establish separate governments? Why will such results follow in the event the Confederate Government is established? Because in all the Confederate States there are ambitious secession leaders who will be aspirants for the Presidency of the Confederacy and to exercise controlling influence in its government and in all cases where their ambitions are frustrated these leaders will cause their respectives states to secede and form separate governments wherein they may be able to realize their selfish political hopes. Within ten years we would have ten or more separate Confederate Governments, which would in time fall an easy prey to foreign Governments. The increase of secession leaders will be rapid and large in all the Confederate States, and their contests against each other for political leadership will lead to discord, promoting continual conspiracies and revolutions, which will produce many Court Julians, or traitors, who will call to their aid foreign Governments to despoil the people who refuse to help them gratify their selfish ambitions.

Never will I consent to give up our Federal Constitution and our union of States for a Confederate constitution and government whose foundation principles of secession must and will prevent its successful establishment; or if it should triumph, its triumph would be only temporary and its short-lived existence end in revolution and utter ruin.

The Federal Constitution, the Federal Government and its starry flag are glorious heritages bequeathed to the South and all sections of our common country by the valor and patriotism of Washington, and all the brave revolutionary soldiers, who fought for and won American independence. Our galaxy of Southern Presidents—Washington, Jefferson, Monroe, Jackson, Taylor, Tyler and Polk cemented the bonds of union between all the States which can never be broken. Washington declared for an indivisible union and Jackson made the secession of South Carolina and of other States impossible. Jefferson by the Louisiana purchase added a vast empire of country to our union, and Polk followed his example by further extending our Union to embrace Texas, New Mexico, Arizona, Colorado, and California. Monroe established the Monroe Doctrine which for all time preserves and safeguards the Governments of the Western

Hemisphere against foreign conquest. All our Northern Presidents have been equally partiotic and just to the South. Not a single Southern right has been violated by any President or by any Federal Administration. President Lincoln has been elected, because the secession Democratic leaders divided the Democratic party and caused the nomination of two, separated Presidential Democratic tickets and nominees.

Both branches of Congress are Democratic; therefore it will be impossible for President Lincoln's administration to enact or enforce any laws or measures that can injure Southern rights. But grant for the sake of the argument that the time may come when both branches of Congress are Republican and laws are enacted and enforced which will injure or destroy Southern rights what shall we then do? I answer that sufficient unto the day is the evil thereof, nor would there be the least danger of the Republican party ever controlling both branches of Congress and all branches of the Federal Government if the secession leaders would permit the Democratic party to remain a solid indivisible party.

But if the day should ever come when Southern rights are ruthlessly violated or injured by the Republican party, we of the South will then fight for our rights under the Stars and Stripes and the Federal Constitution in one hand and the sword in the other we shall march on to victory.

I believe a large majority of our Southern

people are opposed to secession, and if the secession leaders would permit our people to take ample time to consider secession and then hold fair elections the secession movement would be defeated by an overwhelming majority. But the secession leaders declare that secession has already been peaceably accomplished and the Confederate Government independence and sovereignty will soon be acknowledged by all foreign governments. They tell us that the Confederate Government will thus be permanently established without bloodshed. They might with equal truth declare that the fountains of the great deep blue seas can be broken up without disturbing their surface waters, as to tell us that the best Government that ever existed for men can be broken up without bloodshed.

The secession leaders also tell us if war should come that European Nations will speedily come to our relief, and aid us to win our independence because cotton is King and European commerce and civilization can not long exist without cotton, therefore they must help us maintain and perpetuate our Confederate Government. Gentlemen who use such false and misleading statements forget or else are ignorant of the facts that commerce and civilization existed a long period of time before cotton was generally known and used.

They also forget or else are ignorant of the fact that the best sentiment of Europe is opposed to our systems of negro slavery. They also tell us if war comes that the superior courage of our people with their experience of the use of firearms, will enable us to triumph in battle over ten times our number of Northern forces. Never was a more false or absurd statement ever made by designing demagogues. I declare that Civil War is inevitable and is near at hand. When it comes the descendants of the heroes of Lexington and Bunker Hill will be found equal in partiotism, courage and heroic endurance with descendants of the heroes of Cowpens and Yorktown. For this reason I predict that civil war which is now near at hand will be stubborn and of long duration. We are sadly divided among ourselves, while the North and West are united. Not only will we have to contend against a united and harmonious North, but we will also have to battle against tens of thousands of our own people, who will never desert the Stars and Stripes nor surrender the union of states for a Southern Confederacey of states, whose principles of secession must inevitably lead to discord, conspiracy and revolution, and at last anarchy and utter ruin. When the tug of war comes, it will indeed be the Greek meeting Greek. Then, oh my fellow countrymen, the fearful conflict will fill our fair land with untold suffering, misfortune and disaster. The soil of our beloved South will drink deep the precious blood of our sons and brethern. In Earnest prayer to our Heavenly Father, I have daily petitioned him to cast out from my mind the dark foreboding of the coming conflict. My prayers have caused the light of reason to cast the baleful shadows of the coming events before me. I cannot, nor will I close my eyes against the light and voice of reason. The die has been cast by your secession leaders, who you have permitted to sow and broadcast the seeds of secession, and you must ere long reap the fearful harvest of conspiracy and revolution.

NOTE

A copy of this speech was sent to The University of Texas Library by S. A. Hackworth. The *Brenham Inquirer,* April 3, 1861, mentions the speech, also the ominous threats made against Houston's life should he try to make a speech at Brenham; it also states that a "brave secession leader" addressed "the howling mob" stating that he would protect General Houston while he made any speech he might wish to make. But The *Enquirer* did not report the speech or any part of it; but it did give the date as March 31, 1861.

In sending the copy to The University of Texas, Mr. S. A. Hackworth wrote the following letter:

Galveston, Texas (no date).

I herewith enclose to you a correct report of the great speech made by Governor Sam Houston at Brenham, Texas, in 1861, immediately after he had been deposed from the Governorship of the State, because he refused to take the Oath of Allegiance to the Confederate Government. General Houston, accompanied by his family, was on his way, by stage travel, from Austin to his home at Cedar Point, near the old battlefield of San Jacinto. He did not wish to speak, but his old soldier comrades, and other friends at Brenham insisted that he speak his sentiments. He firmly continued to refuse their invitation, until some of the hot-blooded secessionists declared that he should not speak. This aroused the old lion-hearted hero, and he then consented to speak. I remember the scene as vividly as if it had been only yesterday. The excitement was intense; excited groups of secessionists gathered upon the street corners, and declared that it would be treason against the Confederate Government to permit Governor Houston to speak against secession. The court house was densely packed, and as Governor Houston arose to speak, cries were heard: "Put him out; don't let him speak; kill him." At this moment, Mr Hugh McIntyre, a wealthy planter of the community, and a leading secessionist, sprang upon the table and drew a large Colt revolver saying: "I and 100 other friends of Governor Houston have invited him to address us, and we will kill the first man who insults, or who may, in any way attempt to injure him. I myself think that Governor Houston ought to have accepted the situation, and ought to have taken the oath of allegiance to our Confederate Government, but he thought otherwise. He is honest and sincere, and he shed his blood for Texas independence. There is no other man alive who has more right to be heard by the people of Texas.

Now, fellow-citizens, give him your close attention; and you ruffians, keep quiet, or I will kill you." This warning had the desired effect and only frequent cheers interrupted the Governor during his address. His speech so deeply impressed me, that at the time I wrote it out from memory. I gave a copy of it to the editor of the *Brenham Enquirer* (Mr. Rankin), who complimented me on the correctness of the report, but he deemed it inexpedient to print it. I also gave a copy of it to Mr. Hugh McIntyre, and he, too, declared it correct in every detail. I may have failed to use Governor Houston's exact words in a few phrases, or sentences, but my report of his line of argument is perfect. So far as I know this speech has never been printed, and believing that it will be of interest to the people of Texas and other States, to read that grand old Hero's speech, which so prophetically and fearlessly predicted coming events of disaster to our people, I herewith submit to you for publication.

S. A. Hackworth.

ACKNOWLEDGMENTS

Texas Tourist Development Agency, front cover portrait
Wesley Klug, cover art, 6, 9, 13
U.S.D.I., National Park Service, 16-17
Texas History Center, Univ. of Texas, 18, 21, 28, 52, 56, 61, 70, 74, 77, 80, 92, 32
Texas State Library, 21, 87
Architect of the U.S. Capitol, back cover portrait, 22
U.S. Postal Service, 37, 95
Texas State Capitol Library, title page, 46, 48-49, 58
Texas State Dept. of Highways, 41
Tennessee Tourist Development, 63, 66
Allan Carpenter, 98

INDEX

109